Beyond Now

JONAH FONTENOT

Author ReputationPress®
Creativity & Branding

Author Reputation Press LLC
45 Dan Road Suite 5
Canton MA 02021
www.authorreputationpress.com
Hotline: 1(800) 220-7660
Fax: 1(855) 752-6001

Ordering Information:
Quantity sales. Special discounts are available on quantity purchases by corporations, associations, and others. For details, contact the publisher at the address above.

Printed in the United States of America.

ISBN-13:	Softcover	978-1-64961-055-3
	eBook	978-1-64961-056-0

Library of Congress Control Number: 2020902934

Contents

This is the kind of man, husband,
and provider I want to be.

Take Mine

Standing in line
She needed two
But could afford only one

Without hesitation
Softly he said
Take mine

They hadn't eaten for days
And when she finished first

Without hesitation
Softly he said
Take mine

When the wind became cold
And she had no coat

Without hesitation
Softly he said
Take mine

When she needed
Strong arms
To hold her

Without hesitation
Softly he said
Take mine

When test results showed
Her kidney was bad

Without hesitation
Softly he said
Take mine

On a dark winding road
She lost two pints
Then three

Without hesitation
Softly he said
Take mine

When a choice had to be made
And only one would live another day

Without hesitation
Softly he said
Take mine

NOTES:

_____
_____
_____
_____
_____
_____
_____
_____
_____
_____
_____
_____
_____
_____
_____
_____
_____
_____
_____
_____
_____
_____
_____
_____
_____
_____
_____
_____
_____
_____
_____
_____
_____
_____

My father – in – law is a busy man. He worked full time starting at age 10 or 11. He was employed as a sewing machine repairman for decades until retiring in 1997. These days he doesn't move very fast and gets around with a walker. Every morning he gets his hand tools and goes outside to build or repair things around the house and yard. He builds bird houses, clotheslines, tables, chairs, and many other things and repairs damage to things like the porch stairs and makes planters for his wife's flowers or anything else she says she needs. His work is commercial grade but he isn't interested in selling anything he builds. He just wants to stay busy and take care of his wife.

These Hands

These hands have done a lot of work
Protected you from those who are jerks

These hands endured the rigors of a long day
And sacrificed for you in many ways

These hands have fixed many things
And gave your mom a ring

These hands will never hurt you
And will always know what to do

These hands support you all
These hands neither delay nor stall

These hands carry you and lift you high
Caressing your face when you cry

These hands do whatever you need
Because these hands have a family to feed

No matter what happens any day of any year
These hands never wipe away tears

Because I hold in these hands everything I love
I received this all as a gift from above

Many years ago when I folded these hands
I said a prayer so beautiful and grand

God gave me something no one else could
He told me to stay busy and I said I would

I have your whole life and always will
Until the day my hands finally stay still

NOTES:

A fair measure of success considers what one has overcome to reach his current standing. For years I thought I was supposed to ignore problems I was awarded in my youth or pretend I had none. In time I learned to accept my conditions and be proud of my experiences because despite my difficult struggles I didn't surrender and never lost focus. I'm not the only one who had it rough growing up but I don't know anyone else who never touched alcohol or illegal drugs during or following an upbringing that included the same kind of demanding circumstances. So I limp a bit these days and deal with early onset arthritis but I think overall I came out of it okay.

Yesterday

The injuries I sustained yesterday
Hinder me today

But the anguish and turmoil
Will not be for my garden its soil

I fight a monster that intends to destroy
Making me less desirable to employ

But I still work and keep my eye on the prize
I will have to fight the monster every day I'm alive

But that's fine because struggle is all I know
The effort is what strengthens me and helps me grow

NOTES:

_____
_____
_____
_____
_____
_____
_____
_____
_____
_____
_____
_____
_____
_____
_____
_____
_____
_____
_____
_____
_____
_____
_____
_____
_____
_____
_____
_____
_____
_____
_____
_____
_____

NOTES:

_____

_____

_____

_____

_____

_____

_____

_____

_____

_____

_____

_____

_____

_____

_____

_____

_____

_____

_____

_____

_____

_____

_____

_____

_____

_____

_____

_____

_____

The uniform is trauma. This is for those who, like me, bear the physical or psychological scars of difficult circumstances. This can come from how someone is raised or other sources such as occupational stress. Law enforcers for example have a most taxing job. This is especially so these days with anti-American and domestic terrorist groups promoting hatred and division while working against capitalism and our justice system. Understandably these groups deeply resent equal opportunity and the fair and equal application of just law that peace officers deliver everyday often at risk to their lives. This poem is for all who put themselves in harm's way in the interest of serving those in need and recognizes that one need no uniform to know pain, sacrifice, and loss. In fact pets can be traumatized too. All animals can be so affected. Trauma hurts everyone.

I Wore That Uniform Too

I can relate to your sleepless nights
Paranoia anger and frights
I understand why you say what you say and do what you do
Because I wore that uniform too

I recognize the look in your eyes
I hear the desperate pleas and cries
We aren't so different me and you
Because I wore that uniform too

Like you I've seen the ugly side of life
I have dealt with similar frustrations and strife
I can relate and you know it's true
Because I wore that uniform too

I'm familiar with that thousand yard stare
And the feeling of hopelessness and despair
Despite it all we remain true blue
Because I wore that uniform too

NOTES:

NOTES:

_____
_____
_____
_____
_____
_____
_____
_____
_____
_____
_____
_____
_____
_____
_____
_____
_____
_____
_____
_____
_____
_____
_____
_____
_____
_____
_____
_____
_____
_____
_____
_____
_____

My former wife is a good woman and remarkably beautiful. When we married, I had just begun treatment for post – traumatic stress. My symptoms are virtually identical to the most severe cases of combat stress. She found someone who is more sociable and whose family is loving, supportive, and welcoming. I wish her well in her new life. She deserves happiness and peace.

Letting You Go

Everyday you accused me
And claimed we weren't meant to be

You always shared more with your friends
They knew first that our marriage would end

I know I hurt you sometimes
And you were annoying when you whined

Neither of us was perfect you see
But that didn't mean our love couldn't be

You always quickly gave up
When the going got tough

You didn't follow through
With what we needed to do

Except for a decision you made one day
When you said it was time to go your own way

I didn't want you to leave
I begged and said please

But you had enough of my intense behavior
Your once strong love for me had begun to waver

I helped you choose a job for future employment
And trained you well before your deployment

Because this one time you would follow through
Despite how it hurt I was proud of you

I asked you for two important things
One be faithful and two return to me

Despite your convictions of my infidelity
I didn't touch another woman even after you left me

We had our good and bad days
But I was committed in every way

I told you often that I wanted you back
I didn't know someone got you in the sack

You fell in love with someone nicer than me
And you two were quite busy little bees

I failed to make you happy and needed to improve
But I never cheated and always loved you

If you really felt like you had to do it
Why did you choose a soldier in your unit

I served too and can relate to the stress
But don't you think what's right is always what's best

Now you're gone and will never come back
Somehow I've managed without a heart attack

But I love you now as I did back then
And I accept responsibility for pushing you to sin

You don't want to hear from me anymore
So deep in my heart my love for you is stored

Maybe someday we can meet again for lunch
I don't expect it though that's just a hunch

If not it's fine I wish you happiness and joy
May you have a good life with your skinny little boy

NOTES:

NOTES:
_____
_____
_____
_____
_____
_____
_____
_____
_____
_____
_____
_____
_____
_____
_____
_____
_____
_____
_____
_____
_____
_____
_____
_____
_____
_____
_____
_____
_____
_____

Madness doesn't mean anger. Madness means craziness. Anger is a vicious monster that destroys lives. It makes people do and say what they normally wouldn't. It's quite like being drunk but not so deliberate.

Madness

Someone spoke for me

Someone moved my hands

Someone raised my voice

I don't know who it is

I don't say these words

I don't do these deeds

But I said it

I did it

I have no excuse

But I don't remember

I wasn't there

But I was

I don't know what happened

Or why

But somehow I did it

I was drunk

But I don't drink

I wasn't just angry

I was mad

NOTES:

Love at first sight is a rare but real phenomnon. A good man I know recently retold the story of his experience 71 years ago as his wife of 70 years seated beside him rested her head on his shoulder.

I Saw You There

If we weren't meant to be
You could've fooled me

I saw you there
You tossed your hair

The look in your eyes
As you stared up at the sky

You don't know me today
But maybe in some way

Our love will grow
It may be tomorrow

I won't give up hope
I won't cry or mope

I believe we could
And I think we should

But time will tell
And all will be well

For now I will wait
Never closing that gate

To a special love
A gift from above

Someday will come
We'll laugh and have fun

In love we will be
For eternity

NOTES:

The totality of our lifelong learning is impossibly characterized or viewed at once even from the highest point of vantage. Many moments of our lives serve as valuable lessons in retrospect only.

Learning

This is the wind
I feel it
As I turn to face the sun

My senses are overwhelmed
As I absorb my world

NOTES:

NOTES:
_____
_____
_____
_____
_____
_____
_____
_____
_____
_____
_____
_____
_____
_____
_____
_____
_____
_____
_____
_____
_____
_____
_____
_____
_____
_____
_____
_____
_____
_____
_____
_____
_____

In terms of love this is simultaneously the simplest and most complex arithmetic I have ever performed. Illogical and contradictory it is accurate as any definition of love can be.

One Plus You

This one needs one

To make two

Because two is twice of one

But as one I still need one

To be two which is one and you

So if you

Would be my one

And we might be two

There would be no

One in two

But twice of one

In two

That is

Us two

NOTES:

_____
_____
_____
_____
_____
_____
_____
_____
_____
_____
_____
_____
_____
_____
_____
_____
_____
_____
_____
_____
_____
_____
_____
_____
_____
_____
_____
_____
_____
_____

NOTES:

_____
_____
_____
_____
_____
_____
_____
_____
_____
_____
_____
_____
_____
_____
_____
_____
_____
_____
_____
_____
_____
_____
_____
_____
_____
_____
_____
_____
_____
_____
_____
_____

Nothing is stronger or more powerfully binding than love.

Chain Link

Every day with you
Is a dream come true

Every night we spend
Every courtesy and lend

Is special and fulfilling
And continues the milling

Of another link in a chain
Not one of hurt and disdain

But one that connects
To the times worst and best

Binding us together
It goes on forever

This chain is long
And especially strong

Longer than our life spans
It links us to something grand

Every day makes us think
Of our perfect love without a kink

Each section of what connects our lives
Contains three hundred sixty five

Special days and memories
Of joy happiness and glee

I look forward to many more
And whatever is in store

For us in our life together
No matter what kind of weather

Hand in hand we walk along
Whatever the hazards and for however long

NOTES:

Years ago I called my phone service to make a change to my account. The friendly call center agent who helped me became my best friend and later my wife.

The Day I Called My Future

As I picked up the phone
I wondered if my call

Would be answered by someone special
I thought wouldn't it be funny

If my call connected me
To my destined life partner

The call connected
To a friendly voice

Belonging to sweet girl
I could hear typing on her keyboard

As she processed my request
We exchanged formalities

I appreciated her assistance
She was happy to help

I said she seemed nice
She asked if we can talk again

In case I need a friend
This was the most important request of my life

As the years went by
We came to know each other well

She promised to wait for me
Somehow it made sense

From day one
We were never awkward

Now we are married
I recall that day many years in the past

Is the day I called my future

NOTES:

Many of us know someone whose very presence creates a cool place in an otherwise hot environment. Someone whose arrival is eagerly anticipated and whose words, however many or few, are refreshing and restorative.

You Look Like The Rain

Whenever I kiss you
I feel a cool breeze on a hot afternoon

Whenever I hear your voice
I feel a drop of water on my dry lips

Whenever I see you
A big cloud shades me from the heat

Whenever you touch me
My energy is restored

Whenever I smell your skin
I rest in the shade by a river

That's why it seems
You look like the rain

NOTES:

NOTES:

The self-sacrificing nature of true love has spelled the end of many robust men but few ever expressed regret and I can relate because for all I have suffered in the interest of such purpose I wouldn't change a thing.

The Day I Die

Every time she says my name
She relieves my stress and my pain

When she reaches for me
I know with her I should be

She doesn't know what affect she has
This affect is good to some but to others bad

What she does to me takes quite a while
Taking distance from my life mile by mile

Because every word she utters
Makes my heart sputter

And every time she touches me
My heart always skips a beat

She doesn't know I nearly die
Nor would she understand why

But I don't mind going out that way
It's my preference if I have my say

I love that girl more than she knows
With every breath I take my love for her grows

My love for her may grow too much
With sacrifice concern passion and such

I may forget myself and all my needs
But not forgive my own bad deeds

So if her sweet words ever take my life
If the relief I feel ever becomes my strife

I'm fine with that I will not lie
Because I will love that girl until the day I die

NOTES:

I am new to the business of love as I grew up without it but was pleased the first time I tasted it and had a strong desire to sustain the experience. I have stumbled plenty of times walking on this new path but am learning more about the rules of this road and look forward to whatever may be ahead.

Baby Love

A baby need not breathe before birth
The start of a new life
Is a baby's first breath

A need is created
That must be sustained

That is my life

As for matters of love
I was new
At our first meeting
With a deep breath I took you in

Now I can't live without you
And don't want to

NOTES:

NOTES:

A truly beautiful person is also a
truly beautiful experience.

Depth

True beauty is what we do
Not how we appear

The behaviors that touch us so deeply
That we are moved to tears
Are what define true beauty

No one is ever moved to tears
Upon seeing a good looking man or woman

The behaviors are that special element
And indicate true beauty

A mother sacrificing for her children
Or the love of a young child
For his grandparents

That is what touches our hearts

It's the kindness shown by a stranger
When meeting someone in a bad situation

It's a businessman taking time
And turning off his phone
To enjoy quality time with his wife and children

It's a zest for life

It's an appreciation of the truly fine things in the world

It's a deep understanding of a troubled heart

That is humanity

That is true beauty

NOTES:

Throughout our lives we meet people of all kinds. I recall a girl who was deeply disturbed by years of abuse at the hands of her father and later a truly disgusting shell of a man she married. I understood why she behaved how she did and always tried to help which began with getting her out of that marriage so I could take care of her. Unfortunately, she rejected my attempts to guide her any further. As she became more comfortable with me her behavior became more bizarre. Eventually I had to send her packing. About a month later she met and immediately slept with a stranger whom she married two months later. She even called me to brag about her new man. The call disconnected just as I began to explain to her that I dug up some information about her new man and found he was a lifetime registered sex offender who not long before meeting her had served time in prison for raping his children.

Who Are You

I know someone who looks like you
But she would never do what you do

I know someone who dresses the same way
But she would never say what you say

You resemble someone who used to love me
But you are not that one I clearly see

Where that one is now I don't know
People ask about her everywhere I go

She was a part of my life for quite a while
I always loved her grace and style

But you are different this I can tell
Life with her was great but with you it's hell

I don't know where she went or why she left
But I really think she should be charged with theft

Because from the very starting mark
She took possession of my heart

She still has it don't you see
I'm now missing that part of me

Maybe someday she'll return
But not across the bridge she burned

She'll have to find another way
To tell me what she needs to say

But I suspect she'll never try
And I'll never ever find out why

I really don't know who you are
Though you just like her from afar

You wear her clothes and have her name
But she was beautiful and you're insane

So you're not her I know for a fact
And I'd really like my baby back

If you see her tell her please
That I never wanted her to leave

And mention to her whoever you are
That I've been searching near and far

Tell her too how much I love her
And that I really miss my special lover

NOTES:

_____
_____
_____
_____
_____
_____
_____
_____
_____
_____
_____
_____
_____
_____
_____
_____
_____
_____
_____
_____
_____
_____
_____
_____
_____
_____
_____
_____

A stressful and oppressive environment in which one suffers and is trapped develops a sensation of dizziness and confusion. These low dark clouds are not beautiful and can't be photographed. The experience must not be shared.

A Storm In My Heart

Clouds move in low in the sky
The wind blows
The world spins

I know up from down
But not east from west
Or north from south

I feel the pain
I feel the rain
I feel the wind

How can the wind be so harsh
How can the rain be so cold
The pain penetrates every defense

I'm so dizzy
I'm so confused
I don't know what to do

NOTES:

_____

_____

_____

_____

_____

_____

_____

_____

_____

_____

_____

_____

_____

_____

_____

_____

_____

_____

_____

_____

_____

_____

_____

_____

_____

_____

_____

_____

_____

_____

NOTES:

_____
_____
_____
_____
_____
_____
_____
_____
_____
_____
_____
_____
_____
_____
_____
_____
_____
_____
_____
_____
_____
_____
_____
_____
_____
_____
_____
_____
_____
_____
_____
_____
_____
_____
_____

During the few serious relationships in which I have engaged over the years I have made countless mistakes. One might call these love crimes. I didn't know how to love or be loved but it felt better than hatred and I wanted more of it so I kept trying.

Love Me

When I did not know love
But wanted to
I was trying to say

Love me
Love me

All the hours I spoke
Without saying anything
I was trying to say

Love me
Love me

When I was angry
My behavior so wild
I was trying to say

Love me
Love me

When I pushed you away
And complained about everything you did
I was trying to say

Love me
Love me

Now I'm alone
And no one knows
I was trying to say

Love me
Love me

NOTES:

_____

_____

_____

_____

_____

_____

_____

_____

_____

_____

_____

_____

_____

_____

_____

_____

_____

_____

_____

_____

_____

_____

_____

_____

_____

_____

_____

_____

_____

_____

_____

_____

This is my marriage in a nutshell. My wife and I have never argued. She won't allow it. Regardless of who is right or wrong under all conditions she exhibits exemplary respect and will not argue with me about anything. Most of the time it doesn't matter who would win anyway. All that really matters is our bond.

Just Love Me

Love was always out of reach
Until I had you in my arms

When I thought it would last
It didn't

Then you offered me true love
And have always been loyal

Sometimes you don't like me
I can accept that

If you just love me

We disagree at times
But we don't argue
Because I need not fight
To retain your love

During every chat
I always hope
When every word has been said
That you will please

Just love me

You don't have to be perfect
Or always right

I ask only for your affection
And company

I will make it easy as possible
Despite my rough nature

There's no step by step process
Only one thing on this list

Just love me

Leave me if you must
Don't miss me if you don't want to
I can accept whatever happens
If you will please

Just love me

NOTES:

When a man's defenses are finally defeated
by the overwhelming force of love.

Devoted

By your concern I am charmed

By your affection I am defeated

For the rest of your days

I will be here to protect you

NOTES:

NOTES:

_____

_____

_____

_____

_____

_____

_____

_____

_____

_____

_____

_____

_____

_____

_____

_____

_____

_____

_____

_____

_____

_____

_____

_____

_____

_____

_____

_____

_____

_____

_____

_____

_____

A man I once knew learned his wife planned to leave him. There was no animosity between the two of them. They had a good marriage. She just didn't feel like being married anymore. When his wife realized that he knew about her plans she had him arrested on false charges of domestic violence and sex crimes against their children. In the proceeding months she took everything he had. This poem I wrote to help him express how he misses his children.

Do You Dream Of Me

When you dream at night
I wonder if you might

See me in a good way
As I hope you do in the day

When you close your eyes to sleep
I wonder if thoughts of me do keep

When you smile and move around
Are you thinking of our night on the town

What makes you feel at peace
I'd like to know tell me please

Do thoughts of me draw a tear
Or from thoughts of me do you steer clear

When you dream do you ever see me
Do you ever think of what we could be

When our eyes close we see with our mind's eye
Do you then see what makes me laugh and cry

When you bed down for some rest
Are thoughts of me the very best

Do you see me with your eyes shut tight
Do you dream of me when you sleep at night

NOTES:

_____
_____
_____
_____
_____
_____
_____
_____
_____
_____
_____
_____
_____
_____
_____
_____
_____
_____
_____
_____
_____
_____
_____
_____
_____
_____
_____
_____
_____
_____
_____
_____

NOTES:

_____

_____

_____

_____

_____

_____

_____

_____

_____

_____

_____

_____

_____

_____

_____

_____

_____

_____

_____

_____

_____

_____

_____

_____

_____

_____

_____

_____

_____

_____

_____

At different times in life we have all needed a listening ear or close friend for moral support. So many nights I spent curled up in newspapers with a few sheets of cardboard separating my skin from the blistering asphalt. No friends or family. No moral support. During my time in this rough school I learned the importance of self-reliance, strength, and integrity.

Where Are You

Someone will help me heal
Someone understands me
Someone will always love me

Where are you someone
Please help me forget what I need to forget
And feel what I need to feel

Someone please soothe me
Someone please comfort me
Someone please tell me everything will be okay

Where are you someone
I need you here now
Someone please help me

NOTES:

NOTES:

A friend used to speak often of her deep love for a man who always knew how to drive her emotions.

Touch Me

Your hands are like musical instruments
The sensation of our contact is a beautiful melody
Play my music

Your hands are like soft brushes
My skin is your canvas
Paint me a picture

Your hands are like water
My skin is a desert landscape
Wash me away

Your hands are like a passion
My skin is your purpose
Love me

NOTES:

Love can be compulsive because it is a motivating force. One that is never described as pushing apart but rather pulling together.

Compulsion

You are to me what the sea is to a fish
My choice if I had one
But it is all I know

In any event
I must share with you
I can't help it

Everything I see
And everything I do
I need to share with you

Anything that happens to you
Happens to me too
It's how we are linked

Whatever you need
I am compelled to give
I would change nothing

Going here or there
I guard you
As I am compelled

I know nothing else
I choose nothing else
You are my compulsion

NOTES:

NOTES:

_____

_____

_____

_____

_____

_____

_____

_____

_____

_____

_____

_____

_____

_____

_____

_____

_____

_____

_____

_____

_____

_____

_____

_____

_____

_____

_____

_____

_____

_____

_____

_____

_____

However confusing love is, and however risky the investment, I always wanted to give and receive more of it.

Soft Belief

What is this thing you call love
I've heard but have never known

Why won't you go away
Everyone else did

I don't understand why others left
And I don't understand why you haven't

You believe in me
This makes no sense

I don't understand
Please explain it to me

I don't know what to do
I don't know how to feel

NOTES:

NOTES:

I could've addressed this to Gloria, my mother. I also call her Medusa. She was the most violent, sickening, and vile woman I have ever personally known. She destroyed many lives and demanded her victims thank her for it. All did so. Except me.

Standing Strong

There was wind
There was fire

When the fire burned out
There was ice
And more blistering wind

Damn that wind

That was you
It was what you did
It was what you said
It was the rumors you spread

I don't know why you hated me
I don't know why you hurt me

But all your attempts
To hold me back
And keep me down
Have failed

All your attempts
To break my stride
And knock me down
Have failed

Because I'm still here
And standing strong

You made my journey long and difficult
But you failed to break my spirit

NOTES:

In my life I have seen how beautiful and special a mother's love is though I have not experienced it for myself. It seems to be a natural entitlement. One every child should receive abundantly.

To Relate

I have seen a mother's touch
Is soft
Careful
And loves so much

I have heard a mother's words
Are sweet
And beautiful
Like the sound of chirping birds

I have read a mother's love
Is special
And gentle
Like a beautiful flower

But I have not known
Such things in my life
The damage this did
I passed on to my wife

NOTES:

_____
_____
_____
_____
_____
_____
_____
_____
_____
_____
_____
_____
_____
_____
_____
_____
_____
_____
_____
_____
_____
_____
_____
_____
_____
_____
_____
_____
_____
_____
_____
_____
_____

NOTES:

This was the first poem I wrote for my first wife. Her beautiful face and hourglass body made her the perfect figure of a woman. With help from the monster I pushed her into the arms of another man. I reached out to her since but projected the wrong intention so my attempts were disregarded. She thought I wanted her and her skinny little boy to apologize. I didn't get a chance to tell her it's not an apology I wanted but forgiveness.

I Wish I Were A Rose

I wish I were a rose
So you would stop when you see me
Be drawn to me
Halt your busy day to be near me
And peer lovingly at my features of bright colors
If only for a few minutes

Were I a rose
I would make you feel pretty and happy
If any other rose could make you feel like that
I hope you would still choose to be near me
Because no one could love you as I love you
How I wish to be your rose

I long for your touch
If only in death
I would die happy

Pick me then
Pick me
I want to be your rose

NOTES:

_____

_____

_____

_____

_____

_____

_____

_____

_____

_____

_____

_____

_____

_____

_____

_____

_____

_____

_____

_____

_____

_____

_____

_____

_____

_____

_____

_____

_____

_____

_____

_____

_____

NOTES:

I give my wife one of my heartbeats. I keep the other for the purpose of sustaining life so I can meet her needs.

This Is Why My Heart Beats

This is why my heart beats
It circulates oxygen to my brain
So I can think of you

This is why my heart beats
It moves blood to my muscles
So I can work to meet your needs

This is why my heart beats
It times my steps
As I walk to you

NOTES:

NOTES:

For my many lamentations there are no reparations or second chances. I would do anything to fix what I broke but I know I'll never get a chance to do so.

Insufficient

When you wanted me to whisper gently
I shouted at you with terrible cruelty

When you needed a soft and loving touch
I said instead that you need to be tough

When you wanted me to comfort you
I responded by telling you what to do

And when I made you cry I wondered why
And blamed you and claimed that you lied

All you ever did was love me more
Even when I treated you like a whore

I was sick and drunk with anger and pain
But your love poured upon me like the rain

There is nothing I can ever say or do
To make up for what I've done to you

Though with sweet words I am proficient
Apologies and thanks would be insufficient

There is no way I can express to you
Or anything I could ever do

To communicate my deep remorse
It doesn't change the past of course

But now that I've healed and can see more clearly
I ask that you please listen to me

I have to tell you indubitably
You will always have my love respect and loyalty

NOTES:

A hard body, thick skin, and powerful right cross are useless against the overwhelming force of love. What's most interesting is that we often don't know whether we won a battle against this powerful force because it so closely resembles defeat.

Gentle Touch

This is a gentle touch
My senses are stimulated
I am alive

The powerful punch attacks
But the gentle touch defeats me

NOTES:

NOTES:

I've occasionally thought of the day and night cycle as waves reaching a shore. Each day is different yet can be described the same way and every one is followed by another. Every sunset observed by one is also a sunrise to another.

Each Day

There it goes
Here it comes again

The days flow along like the wind
Each day is new and will never be again

Each night is a secret
The sunrise breaks the visual silence of darkness
The sunset is how the day's closing is celebrated

There it goes
Here it comes again

The days flow along like a river
Each day is an extension of my dream

Each night is a quiet song
The sunrise is the whispering wind
The sunset is the chorus

There it goes
Here it comes again

NOTES:

NOTES:

_____
_____
_____
_____
_____
_____
_____
_____
_____
_____
_____
_____
_____
_____
_____
_____
_____
_____
_____
_____
_____
_____
_____
_____
_____
_____
_____
_____
_____
_____
_____
_____
_____

Another poem written for my wife.
She isn't the flashy type.

Pony Tail

Such a simple hair style
Is the one you prefer

Whenever you wear it
I think that is why I love her

It is quite like your usual way
To be modest and not flashy

You are not extravagant
Or in any way trashy

That is why I love you so
And the root of my respect

You simply are what you are
With no need to be decadent

The way you put your hair
Says it all quite clear

Your humility and gentle spirit
Are why I need you here

NOTES:

NOTES:

_____
_____
_____
_____
_____
_____
_____
_____
_____
_____
_____
_____
_____
_____
_____
_____
_____
_____
_____
_____
_____
_____
_____
_____
_____
_____
_____
_____
_____
_____
_____
_____
_____
_____
_____

Anger manifests in many ways. This little story was written for someone who was angry inside just as I was for many years and for similar reasons. This promoted a special bond between us. Sadly it didn't last long. Anger, the vicious monster that it is, will ruin every good thing in our lives if we don't control or dissolve it. She didn't recognize her responsibility to do so and her monster kept breathing the fire that consumed her life and destroyed the best thing that ever happened to her.

Anger

We were well and having fun
The storm came out of nowhere
What I thought was the calm afterwards was the eye

The wind blows again
This time even stronger
For the first time it nearly knocked me over
I said nearly

Our love is stronger
Our bond is stronger
We are stronger

You seemed so dedicated and loyal
I was sure we would last the rest of our lives
The storm has passed and so has the problem
But it hasn't

The storm is encouraged by a conducive climate
I did well in the climate
But now it's so inhospitable

I can't tell if this is a new storm or the same one as before
The white caps indicate good sailing
But you're not sailing you're drifting
Not just away from me but away from solid ground

This makes no sense
There is no truth in a lie
But one does not lie about what one believes

I used to know what truth meant
Now it seems to have drifted away
Not just away from me but away from solid ground
And there it goes drifting further and further away

Thriving in the climate
Laughing all the while
The truth drifts further and further away

NOTES:

A lesson I should've learned sooner is to treat my wife gently. She found a softer and kinder sort of man when she realized I didn't know how to be gentle and that teaching me was a years-long task that she was not ready or willing to carry out.

Gently

Rock me gently
I need soothing

Take me in your arms
And swing me softly

Tell me what I want to hear
And touch me gently

Softly front
Softly back

Gently right
Gently left

Like a raft offshore
Rock me to sleep

Protect me from harm
Love me

Assure me
Promise me

NOTES:

NOTES:

I've always loved the sunset. It is a beautiful conclusion to any day. As I stood atop a mountain one day in southern California I thought about the sunrise I was witnessing from behind.

Nightfall

The Earth makes a turn

A baby is born
Rain falls in the forest
A ship sets sail

Nightfall

The Earth makes a turn

A toddler makes a friend
A flash flood changes a desert landscape
A flower blooms

Nightfall

The Earth makes a turn

A young boy plays a role
A tornado touches down
A beekeeper collects honey

Nightfall

The Earth makes a turn

A young man starts college
A storm develops at sea
Puppies play

Nightfall

The Earth makes a turn

A middle aged man buys a house
An earthquake rocks a city
Dogs bark

Nightfall

The Earth makes a turn

An old man dies
Dry leaves cover a highway
Apple trees blossom

Nightfall

NOTES:

_____
_____
_____
_____
_____
_____
_____
_____
_____
_____
_____
_____
_____
_____
_____
_____
_____
_____
_____
_____
_____
_____
_____
_____
_____
_____
_____
_____
_____
_____

I remember walking the mean streets of my old neighborhood barefoot one day back in the 1980s. The sun was setting and temperature was dropping. I hadn't eaten all day as my search for work was unsuccessful. My female parent imposed a rule forbidding me to be seen eating and most of the time I was disallowed to eat the food in her kitchen so I had to acquire nutrition on my own.

Hunger

I have this feeling in my stomach
It's like a little bug
It's not the flu

I am dizzy
I am weak
I am tired

I smell food
The feeling in my stomach is more intense
The bug is very busy

I don't know who is cooking
I don't know what they are cooking
But I hate them

NOTES:

NOTES:

Walking over hot sand dunes is a good way to describe many personal struggles including work and school. I hadn't learned about the severe corruption of our education system until my first day of school which was my first day of college. Some things still shock me and other issues just never settled with me. I remember a professor telling students about some imaginary political platform change that she said occurred in the US decades ago and that gender is fluid. Ever since my first time hearing that I never have developed a tolerance for it.

Hot Sand

With every step ahead
I slide back

I don't know my progress
Because my footprints blew away

Each step seems heavier
And the glare brighter

My search for water
As my search for shade

Seems endless
In this sea of hot sand

NOTES:

NOTES:

Every now and then God reminds us that he is still around. His activity isn't usually so obvious these days as in times past but still sufficient to convince the studious observer that certain events occurred for a reason of his design and not necessarily as part of any other known natural course.

On The Wings Of A Dove

It is true
That I love you

There is no better way
For me to say

We belong together
In calm and stormy weather

But our love you see
Didn't rise from the sea

It came from above
On the wings of a dove

Even if you're far away
Together we will stay

Because you own my heart
So we'll never be apart

Love me please
You're all I need

NOTES:

NOTES:

Due to my upbringing I have experienced Traumatic Brain Injury (TBI) many times and now deal with a poor short term memory. Some days are worse than others. Some days are very bad indeed.

In The Short Term

Maybe I can help you understand
You see
Time moves one way
Forward

There is
The past
Where time was
And
The present
Where time is
And
There is a word for what will be
That word is
The future

So you could say
There's
The past
The present
And
The future
Even though the future hasn't happened yet and never will

Between
The past
And
The present
We exist

What links our consciousness
Of the present
To any other period
Is called
Later

From the future
Once we've reached an expected point
We can recall events of the past

Some fondly
Some not
Some indifferently

Between
Now
And
Then
Is
Later

For me
There

Is

No

Later

There's nothing to connect
Now
To the next few minutes

I have a future
I don't know what it is
But I have one
It will be there

What I don't have
Is
Later
I'll tell you something now
In a few minutes
I didn't tell you

It's gone

If what I told you
Marks a point in time
And from that point to

Now
Is
Later
Then for me
There
Is
No
Later

Only the future

Later depends on what has happened
The future doesn't
The future hasn't happened

But later
Is different

It is an extension

Of now

Like
A continuous chain
Linking
Then
To
Now

I could establish
The first link in that chain
And the next
And another
But after a few links
I'm at the first
Because the other links
Are gone

This is why
For me
There
Is
No
Later

NOTES:

_____
_____
_____
_____
_____
_____
_____
_____
_____
_____
_____
_____
_____
_____
_____
_____
_____
_____
_____
_____
_____
_____
_____
_____
_____
_____
_____
_____
_____
_____

NOTES:

_____
_____
_____
_____
_____
_____
_____
_____
_____
_____
_____
_____
_____
_____
_____
_____
_____
_____
_____
_____
_____
_____
_____
_____
_____
_____
_____
_____
_____
_____
_____

Hypocritical as they were my parents were Christians. They were members of a church called Jehovah's Witnesses. That church has very strict rules of conduct enforced by social pressure and ostracizing violators up to and including complete disownership of immediate blood relatives. All church members are required to process information the same way and express the same opinions without exception. One such opinion is harshly critical of homosexuals. Anyone who humanizes homosexuals is shunned. I had an awakening years in to my adulthood when I realized approving or disapproving anyone else's lifestyle for them is not up to me. It's not my business. I can only approve or disapprove for myself. The idea of two males in bed churns my stomach but it doesn't mean homosexuals are not people and their lives and relationships don't count. I learned to accept and respect others including those I dislike or who don't accept or respect me.

People

I don't know how it is to be like you
I have never and would never do what you do

For most of my life I saw certain kinds of deeds
As indications of very bad seeds

And while I find what you do to be quite gross
The fact is that everyone has a stake to post

We've all judged others and have been judged too
So maybe I should judge the good you do

It seems quite fair if you ask me
To consider equally your every good deed

So pardon my being so quick to call
Some things you are by no choice at all

But I know now it was more choice than chance
That my opinion formed through simple ignorance

For so long I stuck to my beliefs like glue
But I see now that people like you are people too

NOTES:

NOTES:

We all know someone whose concern was genuine and influence great. I can say this of a few people I've met in my travels. A special couple known for their tenderness, respect, and love for God left a positive impression on me and countless others.

The Sun Has Set

For years you two guided many to the right path
You offered warm love and compassion
To those seeking either

He was the sun on the horizon
And you were the ambient glow
Now the sun has set

But your ambience sustains in the twilight
The horizon still clearly defined
And for those who sought direction
Their paths are well defined too

In the evening hours navigation skills are tested
But those skills were developed under the light of day
For those he guided

That means they navigated according to the sun
And were reassured by your sustaining glow
This has not changed and never will

NOTES:

NOTES:

We all struggle sometimes to make the best expression of our ideas and feelings. Possibly my brain lacks the storage space for the vocabulary I need to communicate some of my opinions and sentiments so I'm often frustrated by the simplest things as I stare at a person, condition, or thing trying to grasp the totality of the circumstances or maybe study the finest detail to cross-reference with my verbal repertoire before putting pen to paper.

One More Word

I have learned many words

But I need one more

Not just any word

But one special and important word

To help me explain how much I care for you

Because I love you more than the words I know can express

Do you know this word

It is the only one missing from my vocabulary

Without that word

I might not be able to explain

How important you are to me

And how deeply I love you

And miss you

And need you

I don't need money

And I am not hungry

I don't need a ride

Or much of your time

All I need is a word

I don't know what that word is

But it is the most important word of all

NOTES:

There is a colorful type of stone or or precious metal associated with certain milestones in an intimate relationship. This poem honors the 50th wedding anniversary of a couple distantly related to my wife. Friendly and welcoming as these two are, after I wrote this and gave it to them they were so disrespectful I rejected invitations to future events they may attend and won't allow them to communicate with my household.

Our Golden Rose

The day we met
Our Rose was Red
I fell in love
With my life partner

For a little surprise
I covered my eyes
When I uncovered
Our Rose was Crystal

I slept at your side
On a cold night
When I woke
Our Rose was Silver

After a long trip
I rested my head on your chest
Your heartbeat put me to sleep
Then our Rose was Ruby

This morning when I woke
I stretched
I kissed you
And our Rose is now Golden

This is our Golden Rose
Going through beautiful changes
Everyday
As we grow together

NOTES:

NOTES:

This is more like a prayer than a poem, I know. I wrote it the day I married my current wife. I really screwed up the first time. With God's help I won't do that again.

My Last Request

I kneel
I pray

God please hear me
I'll not ask for anything else

I'll soon begin a new life
With a new wife

I need your help
To provide what she needs

Give me the strength
And serenity

To handle the most stressful events
Calmly

Give me the wisdom
And insight

To make the right decisions
Every time

I need soft words
To make my wife giggle

I need clear sight
To see what is

I need vision
To see what could be

When we have children
Please give me the patience they deserve

Please award me the focus
To notice every need

And the ability to meet those needs
Everyday

I'll never ask for anything else
Because with my new wife

And my new life
I'll have everything I want and need

But this request
Is for my new family

Because I can't be what they need
Without your support

In every battle
Guide my sword

In every venture
Guide my steps

In all matters
Advise me

Because I am not enough
I must be more

For that I need you
In order to be what I need to be

I ask for long life
To support them

When I die
I ask that I may die for my family

Until that day
I wish to walk the Good Road

That I may live and work
Aligned with your will

NOTES:

NOTES:

I befriended an Indonesian woman who was kind enough to share her wisdom and teach me about patience. One day following a visit with her physician she told me she had cancer and would soon die. We talked a few more times before my messages went unanswered. Her daughter responded once from her mother's account to tell me her mother died. She was close to her mother and was upset about the family's loss. She said what she missed most was her mother's loving touch. I had never experienced that myself but was able to get a pretty good idea of what it means and wrote this for her.

One Last Time

Just search and beauty can be found
It's everywhere and all around

But such beauty just can't mean so much
As your gentle soft and loving touch

It's what I miss most of all
It's why your name I sometimes call

Come back to me I often ask
Then I see you in a passing flash

In that moment I feel your breath
I can hear the last few words you said

But what's missing is your special touch
How long it's been hurts so much

The day has passed to say good bye
For many days I wondered why

I hope you get my message just one line
I ask you please touch me one last time

NOTES:

NOTES:

This one was written to celebrate one of my close friends. She is among the smartest and strongest women I've ever known. She thinks big and is a problem solver and powerful leader.

Great Thinker

She may spend her youth and work until she is old
But the Great Thinker will not lose sight of her goal

With a baby in her arms and the weight
Of the world on her back
The stress in her life won't make her crack

She is the thoughtful type and quiet when planning
So brain busy whenever she is cramming

Her life is a struggle with much sacrifice
To ensure her family has healthy water and rice

With any problem she will tinker
That is what she does as the Great Thinker

She settles issues
And carries no tissues

She does not need them if she is not crying
But for one matter she is always lying

Because when she is alone
She will turn off her phone

Sit alone in her room
In a quiet gloom

She won't bother anyone
Or disturb their fun

Just quietly crying
Then later more lying

I'm fine she says with a fake smile
Hiding her pain and fear all the while

She doesn't know today until tomorrow
If she will survive a long or short while

Every day is a new strategy
To manage strength sleep and energy

But I believe in my friend because in her busy mind
A solution she will develop create or find

In the meantime I am here to help
But I have to ask because when hurt she won't yelp

That's not how she is she doesn't like the attention
She just wants success according to her intention

She will reach that goal no doubt this is true
She will figure out what is best to do

That's what she does best
And why she won't rest

Her powerful mind is her greatest asset
And my best day was when we met

I'm pleased to say she is my good friend
Whenever she needs it a hand I will lend

But she prefers to stand on her own
And speak her mind in her usual strong tone

She is the strongest woman I know
And seeds of good fortune she continues to sow

These seeds will grow in time for sure
To make the legacy of the beautiful Great Thinker

NOTES:

_____
_____
_____
_____
_____
_____
_____
_____
_____
_____
_____
_____
_____
_____
_____
_____
_____
_____
_____
_____
_____
_____
_____
_____
_____
_____
_____
_____
_____
_____

NOTES:

For most of my life I tried to hide my scars and blend in with normal people. Years of therapy have helped me realize that I simply am what I am and so long as I can adjust and adapt I need not present a false front or waste my time trying to blend in with people who are not like me. I was ashamed of my story because of what I have experienced but one day I realized my life might make a great novel or movie because of what I have experienced. It hasn't been glamorous. But looking back I have to admit it has been very interesting and dramatic.

Never Normal

Born of fire and ice
All that is worthwhile has a tremendous price

Every time I looked around
I was on dangerous ground

Each day of life
Presented its own strife

I had to get what I would need
Without compromising my creed

I worked hard every day
And had to carefully choose my way

I made plans for tomorrow
I couldn't wallow in sorrow

I knew to kill only when I must
And always be frugal with trust

To this day the monster haunts
To this day the monster taunts

Hiding at night behind a tree
My death like my life wouldn't be pretty

My head they would pound
But I held my ground

Punished when I wouldn't do it
They never broke my spirit

Decades later
My gait could be straighter

My behavior often wild
Lessons learned in a while

From those who beguile
Comes my uncouth and unorthodox style

A few listen but don't hear me
A few look but don't know what they see

From an early age
There was not a blank page

Medusa had a cold and black heart
I wouldn't have a healthy start

Someone else had a plan for me
Where I should go and what I should be

Though it's been a very rough road
I have not lost my heavy load

Some things I accept that I will never know
But it's not because I was afraid to go

I tried and failed and tried again
I lived a life like a Bedouin

Destined to struggle in the life of a pauper
I will never be wealthy white collar and proper

Still a man I am and one with a story
Of blood and guts but not for love fame or glory

As heat that once burned me rises from the ground
I stand in the ashes and look all around

Looking back at all the chaos and turmoil
At last I accept that I will never be normal

NOTES:

NOTES:

_____
_____
_____
_____
_____
_____
_____
_____
_____
_____
_____
_____
_____
_____
_____
_____
_____
_____
_____
_____
_____
_____
_____
_____
_____
_____
_____
_____
_____
_____

A close friend in Talisay, Cebu suffered a family tragedy when her home and others belonging to family members living nearby all burned down in a barangay firestorm that destroyed 60 houses. Beside her house was a tree called sampaloc. I remember seeing it years ago during a visit. She climbed it many years ago as did her children and grandchildren. Her great-grandchildren have enjoyed its shade on hot days. That tree was burned to a crisp during the firestorm. Many in her family mourned the loss of their treasured landmark. As did I.

A Special Shade Of Green

Maganda sampoloc
For decades we grew together

On hot days you provided shade

In a typhoon you provided hope
Because you always stood strong

My grandmother knew you
My mother knew you
I knew you too
Every leaf on every branch

As children we played together
As we grew I knew I could rely on your shade
When I needed rest

You are in our photographs
Many black and white don't show your shades of green

You were there for my grandparents
You were there for my parents
You were there for me
You were there for my children
You were there for my grandchildren

A cigarette
Or cooking accident
Turned you brown

Now you are simply wood
Shamed
Humiliated
By the disrespectful fire

We lived together
Until we died together

Because when your leaves went up in smoke
So did I according to my wishes

It is a lesson for us all
The strongest pillar may still fall

What we love may change form
Green leaves turn into smoke
But what we loved once is forever worthy

We always admired your strength
But now we seek your scent in the wind

We will not forget the wind on our skin
When we as children climbed your sturdy branches

We will not forget the feel of your trunk
When our hands touched you

Your special leaves of a special green
Are permanently a part of our lives

NOTES:

NOTES:

For me love is not a summer term class but a committed PhD study. I might never be an expert in this but I want to be the best I can be. I have no intelligent explanation for my pleasure. Love is a complicated matter and invites wild drama into my otherwise drama-free life. It is at the same time rewarding and fulfilling. I just can't explain how.

I Want To Love You

Many events are pleasant only because of love
Others are terrible only because of love

An intimate relationship destroys a peaceful life
Somehow in a wonderful way

With all its ups and downs
Life is an adventure indeed

Love intensifies these extremes
I don't know why anyone would want that

And I can't rationalize my own addiction to our love

As conditions are now
Difficult and unstable

To love you for the rest of my life
Is my sincerest and strongest desire

NOTES:

NOTES:

I value and appreciate my wife and marriage. I was doing fine as a single man but my life lacked fulfilment and the substance I have now. A good woman really makes a man whole.

I Cling To You

As if swept away in a river
I cling to you as I would to a tree branch

As if climbing a sheer cliff
I cling to you as I would to a stone edge

As if ascending to the safety of a rescue vessel
I cling to you as I would to a rope

I hold you tight
Not only so I don't let go

But also so you will feel my love
And how much I need you

NOTES:

NOTES:

_____
_____
_____
_____
_____
_____
_____
_____
_____
_____
_____
_____
_____
_____
_____
_____
_____
_____
_____
_____
_____
_____
_____
_____
_____
_____
_____
_____
_____
_____
_____

Every now and then a relationship may experience a sudden change. In my marriage one such sudden change turned out to be good for us.

Something Happened

Something happened
Is it good or bad

Something is new
Should I be happy or sad

Something changed
But I don't know what

Somehow you don't seem as you did
I'm sure it was something I said

Whatever it is I must figure out
Because you're the one I can't live without

NOTES:

_____
_____
_____
_____
_____
_____
_____
_____
_____
_____
_____
_____
_____
_____
_____
_____
_____
_____
_____
_____
_____
_____
_____
_____
_____
_____
_____
_____
_____
_____
_____
_____
_____

NOTES:

_____
_____
_____
_____
_____
_____
_____
_____
_____
_____
_____
_____
_____
_____
_____
_____
_____
_____
_____
_____
_____
_____
_____
_____
_____
_____
_____
_____
_____
_____
_____

I think we have all been in a situation with equal push and pull factors. There are people in this world who will pull others close for a while then with equal force push away those who came near.

Like A Gentle Breeze

On my Face
Your touch is soft
Like a gentle breeze

I remember the soft ocean wind
When your fingers stroke my hair

But the wind never pulls

Like a warm summer breeze
You gently push me away

NOTES:

One interesting point about relationships is how we sometimes remember with tender sentiment little things that in any other context are meaningless. I wrote this one about someone I deeply loved and deeply hurt. Fortunately she found someone else who didn't hurt her and our relationship ended forever but I hold on to the sweet moments when we both laughed.

Your Shadow

You hid behind a wall
And didn't notice the lamp behind you

I saw your shadow
And was ready for your surprise

Waiting a long while I was excited when you arrived

I couldn't see you at first
But knew it was you when I saw your shadow

The light from behind cast a shadow
As you left me

That's why I'm sure to see you again
To this day I still see your shadow

NOTES:

NOTES:
_____
_____
_____
_____
_____
_____
_____
_____
_____
_____
_____
_____
_____
_____
_____
_____
_____
_____
_____
_____
_____
_____
_____
_____
_____
_____
_____
_____
_____
_____
_____
_____
_____

I wondered how an imperfect person could produce a perfect love. One that never fails and endures as it hopes with the strength of high carbon steel but never gets hot.

This Is Why You're Perfect

Love

Empowers and energizes
Motivates and captivates
Pushes and pulls
Blinds and enlightens

Patience

Hopes and forgives
Permits another chance
Sees through failures

Devotion

Binds one to a cause
Is both the purpose and the effort
Carries another selflessly

Respect

Yields and assigns honor
Bows and waits
Is what every man wants
Defines a King

Anyone who establishes these as
Standards can only be perfect
This is why you're perfect

NOTES:
_____
_____
_____
_____
_____
_____
_____
_____
_____
_____
_____
_____
_____
_____
_____
_____
_____
_____
_____
_____
_____
_____
_____
_____
_____
_____
_____
_____
_____
_____
_____

NOTES:

Love, the mischievous pest that it is, presents an enigma producing the impression that somehow it existed in its present form before we did and will carry us beyond now to whatever lies ahead.

Past Present And Future

You're my past
Because
When we met God gave me exactly
What I needed in my life

You're my present
Because
Everything I do is for you

You're my future
Because
Our lives are braided together and I don't want to think of
Life without you

NOTES:

NOTES:

I wrote this poem to all my fellow public servants who can't sincerely promise to be home after work. Soldiers, sailors, airmen, and marines are included in this bunch but the list is much longer than that as it extends just the same to nurses, firemen, lifeguards, law enforcers, physicians, Pinoy OFW, and many other work fields requiring an agreement to sacrifice one's own life if necessary for the promotion of a greater good. This does not honor those who sacrifice for socialism or communism as those who promote such systems are working in favor of evil. The cause must be noble, respectable, and in fact good and those engaged in its fine production are truly heroes and heroines and should be honored as such.

The Greater Good

I spend my days with those in need
They are sick with a new disease

I spend my nights alone at home
Without you my bed is cold like a stone

I can't touch you or stand too near
Just close enough so we can hear

I love you all but I might be sick
This disease you see spreads so quick

I work with the ill and deal with haters
If infected I won't know til later

I took a vow many years ago
That I will never let you go

But these patients of mine need my skillset
It's not that our marriage vows I forget

While I can't explain why I must
I appreciate your love and trust

It's not just my job but my moral duty
To care for the many ill I see

It may seem as though I've abandoned you
When I must do what I do

That's not the case I love you all
But I must respond when duty calls

Because there's more to medicine than needles and drugs
Some people just need hope and hugs

That's why we need our entire team
And many prayers for those in need

I don't know if my job will kill me
I leave that to God for what will be

This one thing you should know is true
I'd much rather be with you

But if we don't do this no one would
So please understand it's for the greater good

NOTES:

One of my business associates was excited about a coming new addition to their family. After years of failure his wife was pregnant. When their son was born there were medical complications that resulted in the loss of their baby 10 days from birth. Exactly one year from their loss the couple had another son. They gave this boy the same name as the first because it seemed evident to them that God brought back what he borrowed. The joy was shared among many for the return of their son.

Born Once And Again

Our little man arrived

Heaven sent

With a lesson for us all

Your strength so true

Something went wrong

What happened to you

On our knees we prayed

For you to stay

Too much to say

Too much to do

We had much to learn

And our hearts did yearn

When away you went

Without saying a word

We were confused and scared

Hand in hand

Our heads bowed

Silently we wept

When our eyes opened

There you were again

A fighter determined

And powerful you will be

A leader of men

In the years to come

We won't neglect the important days

When you were born to us once

Then born again

NOTES:

For many years my brother endured horrible, sickening abuse at the hands of our mother and her friends. When he reached adulthood he was so confused he didn't know up from down or right from left. He was battered and bruised by it all and felt ashamed and hopeless. He had no education or job skills, could barely read and write, hadn't learned to deal with stress, and often exhibited extreme behavior. Life was a struggle for him. But weighed down and torn as was his heart, gold will never tarnish. My brother finally gained traction and is now a minister and youth counselor for abused children.

My Brother Gets High

In the night he snored
She knew it was time
A handful of powder
A careful and quiet step
He turns over
She makes her move

My brother gets high

Waking in a daze
He doesn't know up from down
She wants what he has
And now he is a zombie
Hers for the taking
He will sober up eventually so she does it again

My brother gets high

Ashamed and scared
What is right
What is wrong
Where is the line
Where is the contrast
This couldn't be a mother's love

My brother gets high

The world spins around him
Everything is foggy
What happened to him
Where did he go
There's only one place he can go when
He can't outpace the guilt

Innocence pilfered in the most disgusting way
My brother gets high

As if once wasn't enough
Why must it occur at all
The walls are crawling
The doorknob is talking
The sky is falling
The floor is growing

My brother gets high

He doesn't know where he is
He doesn't know who he is
He doesn't know what to do
There is no escape
Until

My brother gets high

NOTES:

Glyselle Palomar is the girl to whom this letter is written. She likely was excited to meet the Pope and present her carefully thought out question for a wise and insightful answer. After this terribly disappointing response from Pope Francis, young Miss Palomar no longer had anything to do with the Catholic Church. She was taken in by another church in the Philippines. I hope to get this letter into her hands someday.

Pinay Reply

During Pope Francis' visit to the Philippines, he was approached by a 12 year old girl who asked him an important question about injustice.

The girl lived in poverty and said many children she knows find little choice but to rent out their bodies to make any money and even that isn't enough to live on. She asked Pope Francis why God permits this injustice. Pope Francis said there is no answer to that question.

This disturbed me. The Pope should know better. There is indeed an answer to that question. I will explain it here. With enough support this message will reach that child.

Young girl, wherever you are, listen to me. God doesn't like what is happening and he doesn't enjoy seeing you or anyone else suffer.

The reason such injustice exists is not because God doesn't care, but because it is so important that we humans are allowed to foul our lives. It is the only way to demonstrate how important it is to keep God in our lives.

No one truly understands or appreciates hunger until they have gone without food. No one really understands or appreciates poverty until they experience it themselves. And no one understands or appreciates light until they have lived in the dark.

Many among us, probably yourself too, already live in a community with sickening injustices occurring all around and do not need any further injustices in order to learn a lesson. But society needs it. One individual, or maybe many individuals might not need that lesson or might not need it anymore. But that can't be said for everyone. So God does not interfere. He lets us live our lives by our own free will. It is the only way to teach us the error in our ways. He gives us guidance so we will know what to do and what not to do but leaves it up to us to actually do it, or not. That is free will.

Think of a wildlife photographer filming a crocodile attacking a monkey. It's miserable to watch a life ended in such a gruesome manner and sometimes the photographer wants to intervene to save the monkey but can't do that because it would upset the natural cycle that must be allowed to continue.

While many things about people are truly wonderful and beautiful, some things about people are not. Sex and violence are simply human nature. Both are so important to survival that without both there would be no humans alive on earth today. It is instinct and can't be changed.

But it can be controlled.

The fact that so many people don't control their sexual and violent tendencies is proof that they have rejected God. It doesn't mean God ignores you or anyone else. He is suffering too watching it all happen.

Throughout the bible the beauty and innocence of youth is mentioned many times always in an appreciative sense. When this is stolen, a disgusting tragedy has occurred. I'm sure you have seen it many times.

But it must be up to us humans to self-correct and follow God. If we are forced by God to do what is right, we will never learn the difference between right and wrong. We will never understand and appreciate the value of God's principles and the importance of maintaining a moral standard in our lives.

This is good for us but also sad and troublesome when it means those who are truly good are hurt by those who are truly bad or by those who simply don't care. It is even worse when the beautiful things about a person are stolen from them.

Faith in God does not mean nothing bad will ever happen to you. Christians die every day alongside Atheists, Hindus, Muslims and Jews. Good things happen to bad people and bad things happen to good people.

The difference is not what happens in your life. The difference is what happens in your heart and mind during and after such awful, horrible events.

Remember Typhoon Haiyan? It caused severe devastation affecting hundreds of thousands of Filipinos, killing too many to count.

Do you think everyone affected by this was bad? Were they all good? It affected both good people and bad people equally.

What do you think happened among Atheist families after the typhoon moved on? They probably cried a lot feeling hopeless and desperate. They didn't know what to do or where to turn.

The Christians did though. They all went to church the next day and prayed to God. They reasserted their hope and faith in God and expressed appreciation for the things they did not lose.

Atheists don't do this. They have no hope. But those who believe in God have hope and a sense of belonging as one of God's children. They know that even if they die God will receive them in his loving arms and protect them in a far more beautiful place where they will not again die or experience tragedy.

This is what God does for us.

God also gives us all strength to continue. God won't stop tragedy but he gives us strength and motivation to push through the toughest times of our lives. This way we can be demoralized, beaten, belittled, injured, and alone and still stand up and shout "YOU CAN'T HURT ME!" Only a true believer would have that strength and courage and you need a relationship with God to have that strength and courage.

This is what God does for us.

Remember, God does not stop tragedies from occurring but takes care of us in ways we don't realize.

Let me tell you another example:

After Typhoon Haiyan moved on from Cebu and the clean - up work began, bodies of victims were discovered all over. It was very sad. Very painful to see that.

One rescue/recovery team was moving large metal panels in the street and found one whole family huddled together dead. The rescue/recovery team workers said the whole family died together holding each other.

They didn't say how the family died. It could have been electric shock, drowning, or the collapse of heavy objects. No one knows.

But I am certain the family died how they would want to die. Together. Holding each other. Wherever this family is now they are still together and their love and bond is intact.

This is what God does for us.

Not the tragedy of a whole family dying but the blessing of being together as a family all the way to their last breath.

Because God loves us we all must experience the pain, tragedy, and injustice of an imperfect world. But don't worry, it's only temporary. God has a plan for all of us. That includes you, little Pinay.

He will end sickening, disgusting abuse such as what you see daily. He will punish those who spend their time and energy hurting others, and he will reward the faithful and loyal.

This is what God does for us.

Remember, the opposite of poverty is not wealth. The opposite of poverty is justice. We are made to understand, appreciate, and need justice. This is why some things we experience are so hurtful.

Don't give up hope. Don't give up your faith. God is not hurting you. God is the one strengthening you.

Be strong. Believe in yourself. Trust in God.

—Matanglawin

NOTES:

CPSIA information can be obtained
at www.ICGtesting.com
Printed in the USA
LVHW041309270322
714518LV00002B/276